STOICISM

A GUIDE TO STOIC PHILOSOPHY FOR BEGINNERS;
LEARN HOW TO ACHIEVE MODERN LIFE HAPPINESS
WITH ANCIENT WISDOM

Descrierea CIP a Bibliotecii Naționale a României

Stoicism. A Guide To Stoic Philosophy For Beginners; Learn How To Achieve Modern Life Happiness With Ancient Wisdom. – Bucharest: My Ebook Publishing House, 2018
    ISBN 978-606-983-605-7

STOICISM

A GUIDE TO STOIC PHILOSOPHY FOR BEGINNERS; LEARN HOW TO ACHIEVE MODERN LIFE HAPPINESS WITH ANCIENT WISDOM

My Ebook Publishing House
Bucharest, 2018

CONTENTS

CHAPTER ONE: STOICISM, IT'S A PHILOSOPHY? 13
CHAPTER TWO: MEDITATE, ACCEPT 21
CHAPTER THREE: ANGER VS. NON-REACTIVITY 30
CHAPTER FOUR: SPACE AND THE PRACTICE OF POVERTY 37
CHAPTER FIVE: TRANQUILLITY 44
Conclusion 53

INTRODUCTION

I want to thank you and congratulate you for buying the book, **Stoicism: A Guide To Stoic Philosophy For Beginners; Learn How To Achieve Modern Life Happiness With Ancient Wisdom.**

This book contains a detailed explanation of the Philosophy of Stoicism in an understandable and relatable manner. For maximum enjoyment and complete understanding of this book, please read with an open mind.

Thanks again for purchasing this book, I hope you enjoy it!

Copyright 2018 by Zen Mastery - All rights reserved

This document is geared towards providing exact and reliable information in regards to the topic and issue covered. The publication is sold with the idea that the publisher is not required to render accounting, officially permitted, or otherwise, qualified services. If advice is necessary, legal or professional, a practiced individual in the profession should be ordered.

- From a Declaration of Principles which was accepted and approved equally by a

Committee of the American Bar Association and a Committee of Publishers and Associations.

In no way is it legal to reproduce, duplicate, or transmit any part of this document in either electronic means or in printed format. Recording of this publication is strictly prohibited and any storage of this document is not allowed unless with written permission from the publisher. All rights reserved.

The information provided herein is stated to be truthful and consistent, in that any liability, in terms of inattention or otherwise, by any usage or abuse of any policies, processes, or directions contained within is the solitary and utter responsibility of the recipient reader. Under no circumstances will any legal responsibility or blame be held against the publisher for any reparation, damages, or monetary loss due to the information herein, either directly or indirectly.

Respective authors own all copyrights not held by the publisher.

The information herein is offered for informational purposes solely, and is universal as so. The presentation of the information is without contract or any type of guarantee assurance.

The trademarks that are used are without any consent, and the publication of the trademark is without permission or backing by the trademark owner. All trademarks and brands within this book are for clarifying purposes only and are the owned by the owners themselves, not affiliated with this document.

Chapter 1

Stoicism, It's a Philosophy?

The word "stoic" is used a lot these days. Picture the unsmiling man who shows little or no emotion in the face of disaster or the woman that will keep it together even in the face of heart breaking circumstances. That at its core is the general perception of the meaning of the word. Merriam Webster dictionary defines stoic as; a person who accepts what happens without complaining or showing emotion.

One who is largely unaffected by situations surrounding them. The philosophy of Stoicism is of similar beliefs and tenets. Stoicism as a Philosophy of Greek origins is a school of philosophy that grew throughout the Roman and Greek world until the 3rd century AD. It's logic flows from a system that believes that we should not be affected by the situation around us. It simply states that as humans happiness can easily be found when instead of allowing our desires or emotions to control us, we accept the moment as it is and try to find the part we play in society and nature.

Stoicism can also be described as one of the philosophies that champion inner reflection. It asks you to take those negative emotions and situations, reflect deeply on them and turn them into thoughts and actions. Unlike most motivational works and methods of today, stoicism doesn't try to change the negative to positive or tell you to live like the negatives don't exist, it posits instead that negatives exist. Accept them, reflect on them but don't allow them to affect your overall outlook on life.

The philosophy of Stoicism was founded as early as the 3rd Century BC by Zeno of Athens. He thought that letting emotions rule you often led to errors in judgement. Stoicism as a Philosophy doesn't bother itself with right and wrong; such arguments only lead to emotions like guilt or pride which it cautions you to avoid. At first, the original stoic philosophers made Stoicism a religion since they thought that stoicism wasn't based on how one was but how one behaved.

A stoic would always amend his views to suit the world and would always remain unbothered. According to Epictetus

"sick and yet happy, in peril and yet happy, dying and yet happy, in exile and happy, in disgrace and happy,"

Stoicism rose in popularity during the Roman and Greek empires. The other was so popular that Alexander the Great and most of his descendants claimed to be stoic. Zenooriginally thought this philosophy on a painted porch which was *The Stoa Pokile,* which, you guessed it, means the painted porch. The name of the movement actually came from there. As it progressed stoicism became more focused promoting life in tandem within the universe, a life one definitely had no control over.

They saw all beings as material and that all knowledge can be gotten from reason. They focused on truth and thought that true stoicism could only be achieved by a sage who had mastered the art of clear understanding and comprehension of the emotions that came with situations, and one could only attain this by confirming his conviction from the knowledge and expertise of the people in the world around him.

In case you were thinking, "What does this old fashioned method of thinking have to do with the issues of today? How do we apply these philosophies that stemmed from a time so far back? How do we understand a concept as abstract as this without burning the midnight oil (which is pointless as this isn't an exam)?

The next few chapters will attempt to answer all these burning questions in a manner that is easily understood. Actively attempt to describe stoicism in such real life situations that it's application would be easy and in such a way that the application of its ideologies would seem so easy.

With all this, bear in mind that stoicism has been merited for the success of some individuals. It has recently been popularized Tim Ferriss and Ryan Holiday from the USA. They have both credited their immense success to the philosophy of Stoicism as it thought them focus, drive, and understanding of what's important. All it takes is the will you already possess, a deep understanding and acceptance of situations you cannot change. A drive to not let the situations of life affect the out look or the goal.

Stoicism may sound impossible, but it really isn't. Boiled down, it is simply the ability to have something terrible happen to you but instead of reacting rashly from that first push of emotion, to take a deep breath, understand that you cannot possibly change the outcome of it. To accept and let go impossible situations. To strive to live in harmony with nature and forces one can't really alter. Stoicism doesn't teach that nothing will affect your tranquillity. It knows that situations and life happens. The philosophy knows that sometimes a lot of things go wrong without any clear reason as to why it does. It understands that despite the plans made and undertaken, at the end of it all disaster occurs as a part of the human relationship. All it requires is a deep understanding that paranoia and anger only weigh you down. It teaches that instead of carrying all those negative emotions and living your life ruled by them, it is far better to reflect on the situations, accept them as a fact and move on. It teaches you to love life and live it without stressing about such shallow things like impressing others. It teaches to protect your thoughts and beliefs, to train and prepare your mind to best possible version of yourself.

Stoicism is very easy in application. Know that first, understand it, accept it. Now you're well on your way to understanding stoicism. Sit back, relax, meditate and enjoy the ride. Yes, stoicism is a Philosophy. Better yet? One that can be easily be applied.

Chapter Two

Meditate, Accept

An understanding of these pillars of Stoicism is necessary. We'll look at each word individually.

Meditation is defined by the Merriam Webster dictionary as the act or process of spending time in quiet thought, the act or process of meditating or an expression of a person's thoughts on something.

To meditate on the other hand is defined simply by the Merriam-Webster dictionary to mean to spend time in quiet thought for religious purposes or relaxation. It could also mean to engage in contemplation or reflection. To engage in mental exercise (as concentration on one's breathing or repetition of a mantra) for the purpose of reaching a heightened level of spiritual awareness. To focus one's thoughts on: reflect on or ponder over, to plan or project in the mind: intend, purpose. All these definitions were given by the Merriam-Webster dictionary.

In all the definition of meditation there must have been one that sounded familiar or relatable. Meditation isn't only done by that annoying, incredibly flexible yogi friend or by some random Buddhist monks with supernatural abilities. Meditation is also that moment you take out of your busy, hectic, annoying life to just hear yourself think. It is the calm you seek in a noisy place; it is you people watching as you sit by the cage window. Meditation can come in many different ways and stoicism encourages it.

How to do it? It may not be as easy as it is for some people. Some people find it more difficult to relax and find that reflective state than others. That doesn't mean that ability to meditate isn't a universal one. All it takes is discipline and the will (a favourite stoicism term) to learn.

When disaster strikes, maybe it's that promotion at work you weren't able to clinch. Perhaps it's the second miscarriage in a row. Maybe it's horrible results after studying really hard for an exam. Even to things as earth shattering as the loss of a loved one. Stoicism understands the popular saying "Shit happens" better than any other philosophy. It may seem overly simplified for something as complex as human emotion, but stoicism teaches meditation as the first step. When that horrible thing happens, we react in different ways. Often time negative circumstances create negative emotions. If one lets negative emotions rule one's live, they will end up destroying some of the things they hold dear to them. Negative emotions feed on themselves in a cycle that spirals out of control into destruction of self. A scary thought, yes but one that can be avoided with careful conditioning of one's will.

There are many techniques used in meditation. The important fact is that you choose one that works best for you. Find a peaceful spot, preferably one with little interference from the world outside. Switch off phones, turn off computers and alarms, if there has to be music, let it be soothing, relaxing sounds. Find a comfortable position, one that works best, and you wouldn't mind being on for a while. Then just close your eyes. Ignore the myths that that tell you to breathe a certain way, just focus on a spot in your body and breath as normally as you would. Focus on your breathing and create mental images to guide you. Think of the situation you've found yourself. Instead of focusing on the reaction and negative emotions, focus on instead on your life as it is. The goals you want to reach. Stoicism doesn't advocate that you avoid thinking of the bad situation all together. It asks you to reflect on it devoid of all the negative emotions. Instead of flying into a rage and attacking everything in the vicinity, instead of destroying the arrangement of your house, yelling at a partner or other family members, or worse going into a deep depressive state yourself, think deeply about the consequences of your situation. Calmly think. Is there something that I can do to change the situation? Is there some improvement that I can make on myself? A stoic is forever in the quest to be the best version of their selves. They work hard to make sure that their will isn't bent to that of the world but instead flowing in harmony. They believe in forces greater than themselves, the universe, and understand that somethings cannot be changed. Which brings us to acceptance.

Acceptance is defined by the Merriam-Webster dictionary as the act of accepting something or someone. To Accept can be defined as to mean to endure without protest or reaction, to recognize as true. Although the word acceptance has varying meanings, we mean acceptance in the sense of this work as taking the situation as it is. Arthur Rubinstein said.

"Of course there is no formula for success except, perhaps, an unconditional acceptance of life and what it brings."

Life is dynamic. It will change from time to time. That is the beauty and the curse of living. In order to have a peaceful, tranquil existence one needs to accept the situations and curve balls life throws as us with open arms. A full acceptance of thing we cannot change. Doubt it's efficacy? Then list in your head the benefits of acceptance. I could list a few to get you going.

Acceptance makes for a more positive attitude. It creates less worry and stress. Acceptance actually teaches true happiness and peace because instead of expending your energy on trying to change a thing beyond your abilities, you let it go. So instead of feeling happy, you practice being happy. Stoicism encourages you to accept. Set new standards for yourself. Acceptance should be a part of life. Stoics imbibe the culture of acceptance. Things happen, that much is obvious, but instead of focusing on how bad the situation is, Stoics accept the consequences of the situation. It may sound impossible. How does one even control their knee jerk emotional reaction to a horrible situation? By practice. Take baby steps at a time. Let go of past failures and losses. Try to neutralise negative emotions such as anger and regret. Start with smaller situations that hurt less and move on to the bigger stuff. Acceptance doesn't happen overnight. It is a step by step process, one you have to dedicate energy to learning.

Chapter Three

Anger vs. Non-Reactivity

Anger is notoriously one of the most damaging emotions in the human psyche. It corrupts and grows until it consumes, for the most part, all that is good. Anger can be blamed for most of the terrible things going on in the world, from something as relatable and abhorrent as abuse in the home or rape to something that is on a worldwide scale like the tensions between countries. Anger is toxic. It festers if you let it grow. Though we've all, at some point, experienced anger, for a more in-depth understanding, let us define anger in the most simple way. Anger, according to my favourite go to dictionary Merriam-Webster is defined as a strong feeling of being upset or annoyed because of something wrong or bad, the feeling that makes someone want to hurt other people, to shout, etc. The feeling of being angry. A strong feeling of displeasure and usually of antagonism.

There are some words that we grow up knowing instinctively the meaning of. Words that we barely glance at while perusing the dictionary. Anger is such a word. Seeing it's definition boldly written simple words leaves you with the feeling of disquiet. No definition there sounded pleasant. Anger is an ugly emotion that breeds hate. Anger is against all the things a Stoic stands for. It is destructive, self serving and has no function in life other than to destroy. The stoics believe that getting angry will give you nothing in return. Instead, it is a weapon used to attack the people in your life, and when those people aren't there anymore, you turn it inward. Anger births self loathing, self hate, self disgust. Think of all the times you've been truly angry enough to react first and think later. How many times after those experiences did you wish you could take back what you said? Change something you did? A lot of times right? Think now of the ways anger has benefitted you. The good things anger has brought in your life.

If you have to think that hard to recall even one thing, that it's obvious that angry hasn't done much in your life then has it? Have you noticed how draining it is to stay angry at someone? The amount of effort and mental resources it takes to hate someone? How exhausted you feel after each venomous interaction with the person? How you sometimes lay awake in bed at night thinking up ways to hurt the person, instead of spending your time doing something more productive? How has it benefitted you? Anger just spirals out of control, until you find yourself alone and bitter.

Nonreactive, on the other hand, can be defined as of little or no consequence: unimportant, worthless. Non-Reactivity doesn't mean that you should go around acting like everything is of no value or unimportant. It simple means that you take things as they come. Instead of flying off the handle and reacting immediately something happens, take a deep breath and let it go. A friend hurts you or screws up badly? Even if they don't apologise, shrug and let it go. Got passed over by at work for that promotion at work? Find out why you didn't get it, how you can improve and if you see there isn't any room for improvement or a promotion, quietly find an opportunity that works better for you.

A common misconception about non-reactivity is that it makes you a push-over. This is wrong. The fact that you don't react doesn't make you a push over. It's the opposite in fact. It has 's a sign of great mental strength. Only someone who is mentally strong knows that wasting time being angry and hateful at things he cannot change is not a reasonable use of their time. A stoic doesn't spend time emotionally arguing his choices or the choices of others.

They do not waste time mulling over the consequences of past decisions and drowning in regret. It has happened, there were consequences. They reflect on their actions instead and the actions of others, thinks of a way, of there's any to rectify the situation. If there's none, he shrugs it off and moves on.

In a debate of Anger vs. Non-Reactivity, non-reactivity has more points in the pros section. Less time is wasted thinking about things that cannot be helped and less energy consuming because one does not come up with improbable solutions to problems long past. As with all tenets of Stoicism, one cannot imbibe the culture overnight. It must be learned and cultivated over time. At this point, I think everyone would agree that if successfully applied, non-reactivity might actually go a long way to solving some of the world's problem. People don't share the same religious beliefs as you do? No problem it's a free world. A relationship doesn't work out? No hate or resentment, just a peaceful acceptance that life changes everyday. Focus on taming anger by first letting go of the little things in the past that you're angry about. As with other emotions move towards the bigger ones until you let go of it completely. It's not some insurmountable mountain that you're unable to climb. It's really not. One advice remains constant in this work. Take baby steps. Understanding and adopting the beliefs of Stoicism should be done one at a time. Eventually, we can all be sages.

CHAPTER FOUR

SPACE AND THE PRACTICE OF POVERTY

Space is actually an important component of our daily lives. Whether it's mental space or physical space, we all need space from time to time. It could be personal space, a clutter free apartment, or just a few hours of room to do nothing other than breathe and relax.

Space can be defined to be the amount of an area, room, surface, etc., that is empty or available for use. It is also an empty area between things. Seneca, the philosopher in his many teachings, viewed everything with a cost or price, even when it is freely given. Think about it. The cost of every single thing in life is space.

You have a beautiful apartment, tastefully furnished with material things. A full social life with friends and acquaintances from all works of life. A hectic work schedule, with tightly packed appointments, classes, parties or family gatherings. You look around at all this and congratulate yourself on living a full life. On paper, that life sounds great, but in reality, you've begun to crave a little time away for yourself. You need space. There comes a time in everyone's life where there would need to be an evaluation.

"Do I really need this thing? Is it important to me? Can I do without it?"

If you answer those questions honestly, you might find that your life has been cluttered with so many unnecessary things. Things that have just been occupying space with no conceivable function in your life. Often times we drive ourselves to a state of near insanity, putting ridiculous pressure on ourselves in a bid to fit into society's prescribed checklist of happiness. Without stopping to consider in the rush if that's what truly makes you happy. Stoicism warns against that. It is about finding inner peace and equilibrium. Do what makes you happy in a way that it doesn't bother anyone. Be you, be true, societal scorn will eventually fade when the next fad comes along. Society can be notoriously fickle.

Does a 9-5 job make you happy? Or would you be more fulfilled as an entrepreneur? Out of your hundred friends how many of them can you turn to for advice and enrichment? How may can you confide in? The possessions you've gathered in the course of your life, the walk in closet full of clothes, the multiple sets of cutlery, that hoodie you've had for years but can't remember the last time you wore? Do you really need all those things to live a fulfilled life? Once you start to ask yourself these questions, you begin to see the elements in your life that are taking up space. Get rid of those things. Take time out for your better and self reflection, put to good use the space you've created in your life. There's a freedom that comes with space, and on your journey as a stoic, you'll discover more and more uses of it. The importance of space is often overlooked.

Poverty, on the other hand, is a little tricky to quantify. The world we live in today has developed such an unhealthy attachment to material things. The actual value of a thing is ignored in favour of the price tag attached to it.

"Oh! Its really expensive so it must he good."

As if one automatically guarantees the other. Poverty is secularly defined as the state of being poor. Merriam-Webster defines poverty as the state of one who lacks a usual or socially acceptable amount of money or material possessions. Wealth breeds an unhealthy fear of poverty. A fear of suddenly losing everything. The stoics believe that constant practice of poverty especially in times of wealth is a good launchpad to learning to handle difficult time. The insist that comfort is at its origin a form of slavery. When one is comfortable, they live in constant fear of losing that comfort and often resort to drastic messages when that state of being is challenged.

If the fear of losing comfort is what rules you, the stoics suggest living as if you've met hard times. If the worst happens, you're already prepared for it. Most people are under the impression that stoics are resilient, strong and nothing fazes them. That's not exactly true. Stoic, just prepare and live life with the knowledge that the worst could happen. So when the worst does happen, it doesn't fade them. Practicing poverty neutralizes the fear of losing everything. If you already live like you have little, the reality of having little will be easy to adjust to. The worst can happen, and you would face it with calm and ease.

Hard times will come. Being mentally prepared for them would make it easier to weather the storms. As someone who wants to understand the philosophy of Stoicism will first have to understand the concept of space and the virtues of poverty. In the modern world, such concepts are looked on with scorn. If you haven't figured it out by now, you should know that philosophy of Stoicism has its own set of beliefs and norms. To embark on this path, most of the deeply rooted beliefs and ideologies you have should be thrown aside on the journey. Open mindedness and the journey to self improvement is a never ending Road. One that twists and shapes us into (I hope.)better humans than we were when we started.

Chapter Five

TRANQUILLITY

The whole point of Stoicism is to be at peace. In the course of researching this philosophy, one may be tempted to think that peace is a permanent state of being one achieves. Which is possible, sure. Once you become a master sage, maybe. Once you've achieved the ability to be completely unbothered by the situations you face. You will always find yourself in a position that tests your calm whether it's forces of your own making or from outside forces. The true test is passed with each storm you weather.

Tranquillity is simply the state of being tranquil. Tranquil is defined as freedom from agitation of mind and spirt. A steady state of calmness. Imagine peace as the cool, thick blanket you can hide under on a really hot sunny day. It's always warm. Always comfortable. Always safe. Sounds amazing, doesn't it? That's what stoicism promises if practised well. Tranquillity is one of the primary rewards for stoicism.

The first step to this is to protect your mind. Your thoughts and mental apace are as valuable, if not more valuable than other weird possessions. Imagine a stranger walks into your house and you just hand over the keys to the place carelessly to go live under the bridge. Sounds absurd right? That's what we do when we gave away our innermost thoughts and ideas to those who don't value and appreciate our insights. Those who do not add any value to them. There is need to know who you are giving the gifts of your thoughts to. Even the bible agrees on that with its verse that states ;

"Out of the abundance of the heart the mouth speaks."

Are the people you surround yourself with thinking on the same wave length as you are? To achieve tranquillity, you should surround yourself with people who are seeking the same thing. It's a lot easier than conforming to something one doesn't identify with.

Work on yourself. As stated earlier, the kind of place tranquillity brings doesn't happen overnight. Consciously change your thoughts processes to suit a state of tranquillity better. You are your thoughts. Think of each thought as a random puzzle piece that fits into the Mosaic of who you think you are. If one choses to think only negative thoughts, then negative will create negative which will spin a negative personality. Practice instead with thoughts of peace and positive vibes. It creates it's own self sustaining cycle and pretty soon all your thoughts would be thoughts on the bright side.

In order to shape one's mind further, one must see their mind as an empty vessel that will be filled with knowledge but will never get full. Thinking you know everything because you have devoted time, energy and mental resources to improving yourself is a form of pride. Know that you don't know everything, cannot know everything and accept it. Your mind as the mind of a stoic will always have room to improve. Be aware of your ignorance and in that find humility. This is the mindset of most successful people and leaders that have changed the course of history.

Another way to achieve tranquillity is to accept that your problems, no matter how huge they seem to you, don't matter in the grand scheme of things. Stoics compare the universe to the vastness of the sky and your problem to a few of the little stars dotting the large expanse. Thinking about your perceived problems that way really puts things into perspective. Marcus Aurelies said ;

"the stars wash away the dust of earthly life."

Your problems compared to the vastness of the universe is small beans. Truth is whatever you're going through doesn't really matter. Accept this for a fact. Once you do the perspective of your problem changes. If it doesn't make a difference in the grand scheme of things, then it shouldn't be enough to cause the amount of damage it is to your life. Problems are easier to accept once it is realized that they don't matter.

Choose to be happy. This may sound like some happy-go-lucky mumbo jumbo claptrap nonsense they tell people all the time, but it's true. Sometimes things are cliché for a reason. Stoics believe that life is a series of choices, each one you make affects the quality of life you live. You can choose freedom, choose to be happy, choose to he honest, choose to work hard to gain independence. Basically for stoicism whatever goals you set your mind on, as long as you choose to do it then you can do it. Life is only as hard as you make it. Once that basic understanding sets in, then tranquillity will be a much easier state to achieve.

Some of the things that keep us up late at night worrying is regret. While nothing can be done about mistakes of the past, to get peace of mind in the present you have to become the best version of yourself you can be. One of the core beliefs of Stoicism is that as humans we have one purpose on earth. To be good people. Being a good human in this non-empathic age isn't easy. Violence has become such a part of our lives that it is easy to ignore suffering. Being a good person will take practice, see and pay attention to the issues in the world around you. Adapt, understand and help where you can. Work hard, give back, don't waste your days sitting idle on a beach because of self reflecting and inner understanding. While Stoicism posits that we shouldn't be bothered by the activities and disasters of the world, it actively advocates for positive impact in the world. Do meaningful work.

Lastly, handle disaster with grace. Stoicism doesn't measure character by how poised one is during easy times. It is the perseverance and the strength of spirit during the difficult times that shows your true strength. To achieve tranquillity, optimism should be the watch word. Think positive thoughts, put in the energy to create possible outcomes and when all else fails, raise your head with a smile and face the next challenge head on.

Tranquillity is achievable. It is a lot of work, and it takes a lot of steps to get there, but it is achievable. Overall see yourself as a work in progress. No matter how far you go in the philosophy of Stoicism, know there's even more of a long road ahead. Nothing is impossible to do; you just have to put your mind to it.

CONCLUSION

Thank you again for purchasing this book. I hope this book has been very informative and helped you to have a full understanding of Stoicism. I aldo hope stoicism is a path you've decided to embark on. Further research, books, and practices are available to read up over the Internet.

Finally, if you enjoyed this book, then I'd like to ask you for a favor, would you be kind enough to leave a review for this book? It'd be greatly appreciated!

Thank you and good luck!

www.ingramcontent.com/pod-product-compliance
Lightning Source LLC
Chambersburg PA
CBHW070950180426
43194CB00041B/2037